How to Make Kimchi

Everything You Need to Know - How to Make Kimchi at Home, Most Delicious Kimchi Recipes, Simple Methods, Useful Tips, Common Mistakes, FAQ

Table of Contents

Introduction

This book contains proven steps and strategies on how to cook and prepare the deceptively simple dish known as kimchi.

Kimchi is a traditional fermented food that has its origins in Korea. It's known for its bright red colour and its spicy, flavour-filled taste. While this delicious dish is slowly gaining in global popularity, in Korea it's eaten with *every* meal.

This, then, is far more than just a condiment. There are a dizzying number of traditional ways to prepare and serve kimchi, and new recipes are emerging every day as kimchi becomes more and more popular in other nations and cultures around the world. This dish is intimately connected with Korean history and culture, but its versatility has provided a delicious bridge between the Korean diaspora and just about every food culture it has encountered.

If you're ready to start adding kimchi spice to your kitchen, read on!

The Basics of Home-Made Kimchi

Kimchi is, first and foremost, a comfort food. While you can find it in more and more restaurants around the world, it's not meant to be an exotic or artisanal dish. This is a daily food, something that is easy to prepare and meant to be consumed in the home.

There are four main components of making kimchi: temperature, time, seasonings, and ingredients. The combination of these four things is what change the taste, and often make the difference between kimchi that is delicious and kimchi that is inedible.

The fermentation process is easier than it seems, but it requires time, patience, and correct storage. After the veggies and seasonings are sliced, ground, and salted, they should be stored in a cold, dark place for a certain amount of time so that fermentation can take place. You can store your kimchi in the back of a kitchen cabinet, but the best place for storage is the refrigerator, as you can control the temperature. It's the chemical processes of fermentation that not only give kimchi its flavour, but introduce a host of beneficial microorganisms into the dish that make it incredibly good for gut and digestive health. While the kimchi is fermenting, the salt will draw the liquid out of the veggies and form a salty water around them. This salty liquid is known as the brine. Submersion in brine is how the kimchi gains its flavour - if the kimchi is too dry, it will end up becoming too salty to eat.

The containers kimchi is stored in should be plastic, glass, ceramic, or porcelain. Never use metal containers to store kimchi. It's an acidic dish, and the acids will cause the metal from the containers to leech into the kimchi itself. Hard plastics are okay, but glass, ceramic, or porcelain containers are ideal. Always remember to cover and seal fermenting kimchi containers. Fermentation is only possible in an air-tight environment. Long-term exposure to the air causes oxidation, which will cause the kimchi to rot and make it unsafe to eat.

Traditional Kimchi Recipes

Are you ready to start preparing your kimchi? Below are some delicious, traditional Korean recipes that are good to eat all-year round.

Cured Green Chilies

This recipe, essentially just fermented chilies, is a year-round stable in Korean households. Serve these as a condiment with meat, fish, or vegetarian dishes.

Prep Time: 30 minutes

Fermentation Time: 1-3 months

Ingredients:

1 bunch fresh hot green chilies

1 cup fermented anchovy paste

2 cups fish sauce

⅔ Cup chopped garlic

½ cup chopped ginger

¾ cup coarse ground red chili

Instructions:

1. Rinse the green chilies and drain. Set aside to dry.
2. Mix together the fermented anchovy paste, fish sauce, garlic, ginger, and ground red chili. Add the green chilies and gently stir to coat them in the seasoning.
3. Transfer to a dry container and weigh down with a heavy plate. Cover and allow to ferment in a cool, dark place for 1 to 3 months.

Fresh Young Spinach Kimchi

This is a particularly easy kimchi to make because it uses the entire spinach plant. No chopping, slicing, or tearing is required. You can eat this kimchi by itself, or serve it as a condiment.

Prep time: 30 minutes

Fermentation time: 24 hours

Ingredients:

One bunch fresh, tender young spinach with roots attached

2 cups chopped garlic

5 tablespoons ginger

½ cup coarse ground red chili

½ cup finely ground red chili

½ cup fish sauce

3 tablespoons sea salt

2 tablespoons sugar

1 Korean radish, cut into fine slices

1 white onion, cut into fine slices

8 scallions (spring onions)

½ cup red chili threads

Instructions:

1. Wash the spinach well in several changes of water and trim away any yellow or rotten leaves. Drain and set aside to dry.
2. Combine the garlic, ginger, ground chilies, fish sauce, salt, and sugar. Mix well.

3. Add the drained spinach, radish, onion, and scallions. Toss gently with the seasoning mix and the chili threads.

4. Place in a covered container and refrigerate. With a bit of vinegar and sesame oil, this kimchi can even be served right away.

Salted Carrots with Rice Bran

You can replace this recipe with radishes and cucumbers if you prefer. This dish can be served by itself, or as a side.

Prep Time: 15 mins, plus 2-3 days for drying

Fermentation Time: 2-3 months

Ingredients:

2 cups rice bran

10 tablespoons of coarse sea salt, divided

½ cup dried chili seeds

1 bunch long, tender carrots

Instructions:

1. Wilt and partially dry the carrots by laying several together in a bundle and hanging them over a rope or bamboo pole in a cool, shady spot for 2-3 days. This will make the carrots soft and pliable.
2. Mix together the rice bran, 7 tablespoons of salt, and the chili seeds.
3. Bend each carrot into a doughnut shape and firmly place it in a container, arranging as compactly as possible. Alternate layers of carrot and rice bran (the bran should cover the spaces between the carrots so that all the space in the container is filled). Sprinkle over the remaining three tablespoons of the salt. Weight down the ingredients with a heavy plate. The weight is important for fermentation - simply sealing the container isn't enough. Cover and set in a cool, dark place to ferment for 2 to 3 months. To serve, remove the carrots from the container, and rinse off the bran. Slice thinly.

Daikon Kimchi

Daikon kimchi has a completely different flavour from cabbage-based kimchi. Sweeter and crunchier, this traditional dish is called *kkakdugi* in Korean.

Prep time: 30 mins, plus 24 hours for salting

Fermentation time: 1 week

Ingredients:

2 cups fresh daikon

1 cup coarse sea salt

1 cup Korean chili powder

3 cups chopped leek

3 tablespoons minced garlic

2 tablespoons finely grated ginger

2 tablespoons fish sauce

1 tablespoon salt

3 tablespoons granulated sugar

Instructions:

1. Peel and cut the daikon into large cubes.
2. Salt and cover with water. Leave to stand overnight.
3. Drain the water off the daikon. Rinse repeatedly in cold water.
4. Mix together the chili powder, chopped leek, minced garlic, grated ginger, fish sauce, salt, and sugar in a large bowl.
5. Mix the daikon into the bowl with the seasonings.
6. Pour the whole mix into a jar or container and leave at room temperature for 24 hours, then transfer to the fridge to ferment for one week. You can leave it in the fridge for as long as six weeks for a stronger flavour.

Whole Cucumber Kimchi

This kimchi is traditionally eaten in late summer, but you can enjoy it all year round with a bowl of noodles.

Prep time: 1 hour 30 minutes

Fermentation time: 2 weeks

Ingredients:

10 cucumbers

1 cup coarse sea salt

⅔ cups Korean chili powder

2 cups finely chopped leek

1 teaspoon garlic

1 teaspoon grated ginger

1 cup shredded fresh daikon

2 tablespoons coarse sea salt

2 teaspoons sugar

Instructions:

1. Make four vertical in each cucumber. Salt the cucumbers.
2. Place the salted cucumbers in a bowl and fill the bowl with water. Leave to stand for 30 mins at room temperature.
3. Rinse the salt off.
4. Mix the chili powder, leek, garlic, ginger, daikon, salt, and sugar in a separate bowl.
5. Mix the cucumbers into the seasoning bowl.
6. Pack the cucumbers together tightly in a jar or other container, then transfer to the fridge for 2 weeks to ferment.

Easy Traditional Kimchi Recipes

If you're on a tight schedule or budget, don't worry. These recipes are both traditional and simple to prepare, with low-cost ingredients and a quick fermentation time.

Fresh Ginger Pickles

This dish is definitely a condiment, rather than a side.
Serve with steamed meat, chicken, or fish.

Prep time: 30 mins, plus ½ hour for salting

Fermentation time: 1-2 weeks

Ingredients:

2 cups fresh ginger, peeled

5 tablespoons coarse sea salt

5 tablespoons sugar

2 cups water

½ tablespoons ascorbic acid (Vitamin C1, granules or powder)

1 tablespoon white vinegar

Instructions:

1. Place the ginger slices in a clean, dry container. Add the salt and sugar and mix well. Let this stand for 30 minutes.
2. Add the water, Vitamin C1, and vinegar to the container and stir to mix.
3. Cover and let the pickle ferment for 1-2 weeks in the fridge. This will yield a fresh, ginger flavour. If you let it ferment longer than 2 weeks, you will get a more intense (but still delicious) pickle.

Stuffed Green Cabbage Kimchi

This kimchi can be eaten by itself, and only need a few days to ferment.

Prep time: 30 mins, plus 1-2 hours for brining

Fermentation time: 2 days

Ingredients:

1 head green cabbage

8 tablespoons coarse sea salt, divided

4 cups water

3 Korean radishes, cut into thin slices

⅔ Cup chopped garlic

5 tablespoons chopped ginger

⅔ Cup fish sauce

½ cup coarse ground red chili

½ cup finely ground red chili

2 tablespoons sugar

12 scallions (spring onions) cut into thin slices

½ cup red chili threads

Instructions:

1. Remove 12 outer leaves from the cabbage. In a medium bowl, combine 5 tablespoons of the salt with 3 cups of the water. Soak the cabbage leaves in the brine for 1 to 2 hours.
2. Remove the core of the cabbage. Slice the inner leaves finely and place in a bowl. Combine 1 tablespoon of the salt with the remaining 1 cup water and pour over the small leaves.
3. Add the cut radish to the finely sliced leaves, along with the remaining 2 tablespoons of the

salt. Mix well. Do not drain away any of the brine.

4. In a separate bowl, combine the garlic, ginger, fish sauce, ground chilies, and sugar. Add the sliced cabbage and radish mixture to the filling, then stir in the scallions and red chili threads.

5. Rinse and drain the large cabbage leaves. Place one leaf on a flat surface and place 3 heaping tablespoons of the filling along the centre rib of the leaf. Then roll it sideways, from left to right. Be sure to roll side to side, not from the top to the bottom of the leaf. Repeat with the remaining filling and leaves.

6. Arrange all the stuffed rolls neatly in a crock. Pour the reserved liquid from the radishes over and add enough water to just cover, then weigh down with a plate or saucer. The weight is important for fermentation - simply sealing the crock isn't enough. Allow to ferment lightly for 2 days, or serve immediately with a splash of vinegar.

Juicy Green Cabbage Kimchi

In the fall, winter, and spring, serve this kimchi with cold noodles; in the summer, with cold rice. This kimchi should be served wet, with a liberal serving of the brine.

Prep time: 30 mins

Fermentation time: 2 days

Ingredients:

2 teaspoons rice flour

3 cups water

1 large head green cabbage

2 cups Korean watercress

7 tablespoons coarse sea salt, divided

⅔ Cup chopped garlic

½ cup chopped ginger

½ cup fresh red chili, seeded

½ cup cooked shelled chestnuts, finely sliced

16 scallions (spring onions)

5 cups water

Instructions:

1. Combine the rice flour and ½ cup water in a small saucepan over medium-low heat. Bring to a boil, and set aside to cool.
2. Toss the cabbage and watercress with 4 tablespoons of the salt. Place in a separate container.
3. Add the cooled rice gruel, garlic, ginger, red chili, sliced chestnuts, scallions, and the remaining 3 tablespoons of salt. Pour the 5 cups of water over all. Cover, then shake the container to distribute the seasonings evenly. Ferment lightly for 2 days in warm weather. Serve alongside any cold noodle dish.

White Kimchi

Not all kimchi is spicy hot. Before chilies were introduced to Korea by the Portuguese, people were making "white" kimchi. So if you don't like spicy foods, this traditional variation is perfect for you.

Prep time: 30 mins, plus 6 hours for salting

Fermentation time: 2 weeks

Ingredients:

1 large head Chinese leaf cabbage

2 cups coarse sea salt

2 cups finely shredded leek

1 tablespoon minced garlic

2 cups finely shredded ginger

1 red chili

3 tablespoons salt

4 cups water

Instructions:

1. Halve the Chinese leaf lengthwise. Salt and cover with water. Leave to stand for six hours.
2. Rinse the Chinese leaf repeatedly in cold water.
3. To make the brine, add the three tablespoons salt to the water and bring to a boil. Leave to cool.
4. Mix together shredded leek, minced garlic, and shredded ginger. Spread the mix between each leaf. Pack the Chinese leaf in a jar or other container.
5. Pour the brine into the container with the packed cabbage and add the whole chili. Place a weight or heavy plate on top, then transfer to the fridge to ferment for two weeks. You can let it ferment for as long as six weeks for a stronger flavour.

Useful Tips for Optimal Kimchi Preparation

Fermentation is the essence of kimchi creation. Without proper fermentation, you have something that's still tasty, but definitely not the addictively spicy flavour of kimchi. Fermentation is also what gives kimchi its nutritional benefits. Fermentation allows for probiotics and other beneficial organisms to grow inside the veggies and the brine. This might sound a little gross, but these bacteria actually do a lot of good work for the gut and digestive tract.

Fermentation is what can make or break your kimchi, so if you're struggling to improve the flavour of your homemade dishes, it probably has more to do with how you're fermenting than it does with the ingredients you're using. While most people, especially in the west, choose glass containers for fermentation, the best choice for kimchi is actually ceramic containers. The traditional pot for kimchi fermentation is called an onggi crock, and, believe it or not, you can taste the difference between kimchi that's been fermented in glass and kimchi that's been fermented in an onggi or ceramic crock. Why? Because when kimchi is fermenting, certain gases build up in the container that, in a glass container, are only released when you open the lid. The build-up of these gasses is not harmful, and won't ruin the kimchi's flavour. But ceramic crocks have tiny, microscopic pores, which means that the gases be released during the fermentation process. This leads to a better balance of flavour, and kimchi that tastes stronger, but without the bitterness that you sometimes get with glass containers.

Another important step in kimchi fermentation is weight. It's not enough to simply seal the container; often, kimchi recipes will ask you to weigh down the food in the crock with a heavy plate. This is important, as it keeps the solid food submerged in the brine and saturates the food with the brine's spicy flavour. It's also important to remember that your kimchi should be exposed to the air as little as possible while it's in storage. The more air it's exposed to, the more likely it is to stop fermenting and start rotting. So if you take out your kimchi to eat, but you only eat half the crock, transfer your kimchi into a smaller container before you put it back in storage.

How you store your kimchi is also important. A cool, dark space is necessary for the right bacteria to grow as your kimchi ferments. The back of a dark kitchen cupboard or a shelf in the cellar can be great places to store your kimchi. Many Korean homes have a designated fridge specifically for storing kimchi. If you want to really commit, a mini-fridge just for kimchi fermentation can make your life a lot easier.

Modern Kimchi Recipes

These recipes are less traditional, but still delicious, and relatively easy to make.

Chinese Leaf Kimchi

This is probably the common kimchi recipe today. When you see "kimchi" on a restaurant menu, this is usually the kind of kimchi they're referring to.

Prep time: 1 day

Fermentation time: 10 days

Ingredients:

1 large head Chinese leaf cabbage

2 cups sea salt

1 ½ cups Korean chili powder

3 cups finely chopped leek

3 tablespoons garlic

2 tablespoons grated ginger

2 cups fresh daikon, shredded

1 tablespoon anchovy paste

2 tablespoons salt

1 tablespoon sugar

Instructions:

1. Cut the cabbage in half and place the halves in a bowl. Salt the leaves of the cabbage.
2. Submerge the salted cabbage in cold water and place a heavy plate over the bowl. Let sit at room temperature for 24 hours.
3. Rinse and drain the cabbage in cold water, and squeeze any excess water out of the leaves.

4. Mix all of the seasonings together in a separate bowl until they form a thick paste.
5. Thoroughly coat the cabbage leaves in the seasonings paste.
6. Roll up the seasoned cabbage leaves and place them in a jar or crock. Let sit at room temperature for 24 hours, then transfer to the fridge to ferment for 10 days.

Baby Daikon Kimchi

This kimchi gets a fresh, earthy flavour from the daikon root that balances out the spicy tang from the chilies.

Prep time: 30 mins, plus a few hours for salting

Fermentation time: 1 week

Ingredients:

2 cups fresh baby daikon, preferably with leaves

2 cups coarse sea salt

2 cups rice water

2 sliced red chilies

8 sliced scallions

1 whole garlic bulb

½ cup shredded ginger

1 cup coarse sea salt

4 cups water

Instructions:

1. Boil 1 tablespoon cooked short grain rice in approximately 200ml water until you have a white, cloudy liquid. Drain off the rice grains.
2. Wash the daikon and pick off the rougher leaves.
3. Place the daikon in a bowl, salt, and let stand for a few hours. Then rinse a few times in cold water.
4. Combine the red chilies, scallions, garlic bulb, shredded ginger, sea salt, and water in a separate bowl to make the brine. Place the daikon in a jar or container with a tight fitting lid and pour over the brine. Store in the fridge. It will be ready after about one week, but can

ferment for several weeks if you want a stronger flavour.

Squash Kimchi

Gourd-based kimchis are becoming a popular choice in Europe and the Americas for the fall season. Gourds are a staple in traditional Korean cuisine, so feel free to enjoy this squash kimchi all year round.

Prep time: 11 hours

Fermentation time: 3 weeks

Ingredients:

Approximately 1 large muscat or butternut squash

4 cups coarse sea salt

1 large head Chinese leaf cabbage

⅔ Cup Korean chili powder

2 cups finely chopped leek

1 teaspoon garlic

1 teaspoon grated ginger

3 tablespoons salt

2 teaspoons sugar

Instructions:

1. Peel the squash and chop it into small pieces. Salt the pieces. Leave to stand for 10 hours at room temperature.
2. Rinse the squash pieces in cold water and carefully pat dry with a paper towel.
3. Chop the Chinese leaf cabbage into small pieces. Mix the chili powder, leek, garlic, ginger, salt, and sugar together in a separate bowl until they've formed a seasonings paste.
4. Mix the squash and chopped cabbage into the bowl of seasonings paste. Pour everything into a jar or other container, and leave to stand for 24 hours at room temperature.
5. Transfer to the fridge to ferment for 3 weeks.

Easy Kimchi

A quick, modern take on the classic Chinese leaf, this is a great recipe for kimchi beginners.

Prep time: 30 mins, plus 8 hours for salting

Fermentation time: 3 months

Ingredients:

1 large Napa cabbage

½ cup sea salt

2 cups daikon radish, cut into strips

1 bunch scallions

1 tablespoon fresh ginger, sliced (2-3 pieces)

6 cloves garlic

1 shallot

6 tablespoons Korean-style red pepper flakes

2 tablespoons fermented anchovy paste

2 teaspoons granulated sugar

Instructions:

1. Cut the cabbage into small pieces and place it in a bowl. Salt the cabbage. Add enough cool water to cover the salted cabbage. Place a heavy plate over the bowl and let stand at room temperature for 8 hours.
2. Rinse the cabbage and place it back in the bowl. Slice and add the daikon radish and scallions.
3. Blend the ginger, garlic, shallot, red pepper flakes, anchovy paste and sugar in a food processor or blender.
4. Spread the blended seasonings mix over the cabbage. Mix with the cabbage and daikon slices until well coated.

5. Pack the cabbage into a large jar or a crock. Add a little of the salt water brine to just cover the vegetables.
6. Cover loosely with a lid and transfer to the fridge to ferment for 3 months.

Common Kimchi Mistakes

The number one mistake that people make when making kimchi is not weighing down the kimchi before they put it in storage. Most recipes will call for the kimchi to be weighed down with a heavy plate before it does into storage. This weight ensures that the veggies stay completely submerged in the brine while they ferment. Exposure to the air can cause the kimchi to putrefy, and make it unsafe to eat.

Another common kimchi mistake is storing the kimchi in temperatures that are too cold. The freezer, for example, would be too cold. Frigid temperatures are good for storage because most bacteria can't grow in freezing cold temperatures. However, when fermenting your kimchi, there are certain bacteria that you want to grow - without those bacteria, fermenting can't take place. So make sure that your storage space is cool and dark, like a cellar, the back of a kitchen cabinet, or the refrigerator.

When recipes call for "salt," don't use table salt. Processed salt has added chemicals or preservatives that will prevent your kimchi from fermenting. Sea salt, Himalayan pink salt, and kosher salt are the best, but any whole salts that haven't been processed are just fine.

Because our contemporary diets are saturated with salts and sugars, many people try to get away with using less than the recipe calls for when they start making kimchi. Resist this temptation. Salt is an integral part of the fermentation process, and important for flavour. Don't be afraid of salt when you are making kimchi - the bacterial cultures and chemical changes in the veggies instigated by it are incredibly good for your gut health, and will make your kimchi much tastier!

Kimchi FAQs

How do I calculate how much of every ingredient I use based on the amount of cabbage I actually have?

The specified amounts for ingredients in kimchi recipes are about ensuring the flavour properly permeates the brine. So if you have less (or more) cabbage than the recipe calls for, don't worry! You'll still be saturating it in the brine for the same amount of time. The only ingredient to adjust based on your cabbage (or whatever the base veggie is) amount is salt. If you have less cabbage than the recipe calls for, use less salt. If you have more, use more. It doesn't have to be an exact calculation, but too much salt will dry out the kimchi. Too little will stop it from fermenting properly.

Is wearing gloves really that important for making kimchi?

Most kimchi cookbooks insist on wearing gloves because of the chilies. You don't need gloves, but you'll regret not having them if you accidentally rub some of the hot oils into your eyes. Long-term exposure to hot chili oils can also irritate the skin of your hands. Making kimchi every once in a while with bare hands is perfectly fine, but if kimchi is something you think you'll be making often, it's best to get yourself a pair of gloves.

Do I have to use a fermentation crock to make kimchi?

If you want the best flavour, then a fermentation crock is the best choice. That being said, many people make delicious kimchis in glass jars. Mason jars, in particular, are a popular choice because they're easy to buy and store.

Where can I buy an affordable fermentation crock?

Korea isn't the only East Asian culture with a long history of veggie ferments in its cuisine. If you live close to a Chinese or Japanese community, or an Asian market, it should be very easy to find an affordable fermentation crock. Central and Eastern European cuisines also have ferments (think sauerkraut, mustards, relishes, etc.), and so European markets often have fermentation crocks as well.

If you don't live in an East Asian community or cultural market, you can always go online. There are a huge variety of fermentation crocks available for purchase online. You don't need a fancy crock to make good kimchi, so stick to your budget, and find something that meets your needs.

How do I know when kimchi is done fermenting?

What makes kimchi so easy to make versus other kinds of ferments is that kimchi is safe (and relatively tasty) to eat immediately. You don't technically have to ferment kimchi but, of course, that's where its signature flavour and texture come from. Fermentation is also what makes kimchi not just good, but great for your health. The provided fermentation time in the recipe should be seen as a guide toward optimal flavour, rather than the time at which it's "safe" to eat. Once you approach the recommended fermentation time, the best thing to do is start smelling and tasting your kimchi. If you like the taste, go ahead and serve it. If you want it to be a bit stronger, let it ferment longer. If something has gone wrong - for example, if your kimchi has spoiled - you'll smell it immediately, so a quick smell of your kimchi can tell you if it's still good to eat.

Conclusion

I hope this book was able to help you to start making your own homemade kimchi.

The next step is to prep your kitchen. Choose where and how you're going to store your kimchi. Determine if you have the right containers, or if you'll have to buy them. If you don't have a pair of plastic gloves, put that on your shopping list as well. Once you have a cool, dark storage space, ceramic or glass containers for fermentation, and a pair of gloves, you're ready to try your first recipe!

Some ferments are trickier than others. Homemade miso, tofu, natto, krauts, and kombuchas all require very specific temperatures, environments, and are easy to ruin during fermentation. Not so for kimchi! You may not get it right the first few times, but that's ok. Like all foods, kimchi takes practice to perfect. The thing to remember is that this is not a specialty dish. Like mac n' cheese or apple pie, kimchi is something that reminds Koreans of home. With a little practice, this dish can easily become a healthy and delicious part of your home-cooking as well.

The recipes in this book are both common and traditional, with flavours that are basic, familiar, and easy to recognise. But these recipes are just here to get you started. Once you've mastered a few of these recipes, you can start to experiment to make more diverse and interesting kimchi. There are thousands of recipes online, written by people who are native Koreans, Korean expats, and people with Korean ancestry. If you are reading this book to get in better touch with your own Korean heritage, or connect with your Korean friends, then you have access to the most valuable resource of all. Every traditional Korean household has its own kimchi recipes, techniques, and secrets. Share your kimchi with the Koreans in your life, and get some valuable tips, tricks, ideas, and suggestions that have their roots in thousands of years of cultural traditions.

Printed in Great Britain
by Amazon

61320969R00031